THE

Hungerpots

COOKBOOK

HarperCollins*Publishers*
1 London Bridge Street
London SE1 9GF

www.harpercollins.co.uk

First published by HarperCollins*Publishers* 2020

10 9 8 7 6 5 4 3 2 1

© HarperCollins*Publishers* 2020

Photographer: Charlotte Bland
Food Stylist: Pippa Leon
Prop Stylist: Olivia Wardle

Bethie Hungerford asserts the moral right to be identified as the
author of this work

A catalogue record of this book is available from the British Library

HB ISBN 978-0-00-835690-3
EB ISBN 978-0-00-835691-0

Printed and bound in Latvia

MIX
Paper from
responsible sources
FSC™ C007454

FSC
www.fsc.org

This book is produced from independently certified FSC™ paper
to ensure responsible forest management.

For more information visit: www.harpercollins.co.uk/green

THE
Hungerpots
COOKBOOK

BETHIE HUNGERFORD

HarperCollins*Publishers*

Contents

Introduction

If you are the kind of person who has the skill and time to make a croquembouche from scratch then put this cookbook down. It isn't for you. However, if you are the kind of person who loves delicious, wholesome, homemade food, but perhaps lacks the time or skill to make it happen, this book is for you! Quick! Buy it before that chick behind you grabs the last copy!

My 'hungerpot' method of cooking is basically the laziest possible way to cook delicious homemade food. Aside from a bit of chopping and stirring, there is absolutely zero ability required. I promise. This book is perfect for busy parents, university students, for cooking in a camper van, a boat, or over a campfire, cooking during a kitchen renovation, or in a tiny kitchen without an oven. The recipes are also straightforward enough to leave for a teenage babysitter to make or to send to your twenty-something nephew who is attempting his first dinner party. Nearly every single recipe in this book includes a protein, vegetable and starch, making it a complete meal. All recipes serve four people and there is no need to make a side dish of any sort and no need to separately steam your veg. It is all done together!

Although these recipes are embarrassingly easy, I promise they are also absolutely delicious and beautiful enough to serve to guests. So put on some music, pull out that cast-iron pot and get ready to revolutionise your mealtimes!

Lots of love,

Bethie
@hungermama

Casseroles
one-dish meals

CANDY

CAKES and PASTRIES

CASSEROLES

Kielbasa Skillet Stew (used Eckrich)
... onion strips.   (Be sure to read directions 4
...ed onion chopped (or more)   making)
...1/2 lb. smoked kielbasa, thinly sliced
...used all beef Eckrich smoked sausage.)
...(16 1/2 oz each) Great Northern beans (undrained)
...(8 oz ea.) tomato sauce (I used 1 can or ...)
... 1 can chopped green chilies but I
...tom.) 2 med carrots (sliced 1/2 med grey pep...
... seasoning (I used oregano)
g

Useful Advice

CROCKERY

While many of these dishes can be made in a regular pot, some of them do require that your pot is also ovenproof. For this reason, I tend to do my hungerpots in a cast-iron pot or pan, though you can always decant the finished dish into something ovenproof before putting in the oven if need be. It means a second dish to clean, but is still a quick-and-easy meal to make!

If you are in the market for a cast-iron pot, I would suggest asking around for a used one before buying new. It is quite likely a friend or relative has a disused one they would be willing to part with! Otherwise, there are a few grocery stores and department stores that sell cast-iron crockery and they often come on sale.

PERSONALISATION

There is some space at the end of the book for your own notes, where I hope you will record your personal preferences, such as 'double the garlic in the Picadillo', 'try the Mac and Cheese with smoked Gouda instead of Cheddar', etc., and your preferred cooking times. These recipes are very easily adapted, so if you prefer broccoli to asparagus, or beef to chicken, or want to substitute vegan cheese, go for it. Though when swapping veg, do make sure they have a similar cooking time. Similarly, in most recipes I have suggested several ways to garnish the finished dish but there's no need to feel bound by this – just choose whatever you like or have to hand.

SLOW COOKER AND INSTANT POT

Because these are all one-pot meals, they are also easy to cook in the slow cooker and Instant Pot. Just be sure that any 'Finishing Touches' (that go in after an initial cook) are accounted for and added later. That being said, nearly all of these dishes cook in about 20 minutes, so you may be better off just prepping everything ahead of time (keeping the liquid separate) and heating it all up together when you're ready to eat!

Pasta

Minestrone

MAIN INGREDIENTS

2 litres (70fl oz) fresh
   chicken or vegetable broth
200g (7oz) shell pasta
2 carrots, chopped
2 celery sticks, chopped
2 garlic cloves, minced
1 onion, chopped
100g (3½oz) green
   beans, chopped
100g (3½oz) courgettes,
   chopped
400g (14oz) tin kidney
   beans, drained
400g (14oz) tin chopped
   tomatoes
1 tablespoon tomato purée
1 sprig of fresh rosemary
1 sprig of fresh thyme
1 tablespoon olive oil
3 tablespoons red pesto
salt and pepper, to taste

FINISHING TOUCHES

150g (5oz) frozen peas
large handful of spinach,
   chopped
Parmesan cheese, chopped
   fresh parsley, to garnish

This classic tomato-based soup is so hearty that even the biggest carnivore you know won't miss the meat! Full of veg and fresh herbs, this dish is best served with a generous helping of grated Parmesan and a hunk of crusty bread.

1. Add all the main ingredients to a large pot and bring to the boil, then reduce to a medium heat and cook, stirring often.

2. Once the pasta is al dente and the veg is cooked (approximately 15 minutes after boiling), add the peas and spinach and stir until the peas have defrosted. Garnish and serve.

Chicken Soup

MAIN INGREDIENTS

2 litres (70fl oz) fresh
chicken broth

200g (7oz) pearl/Israeli/
giant couscous (do not use
regular couscous!)

1 chicken breast
(approximately 150g/5oz)

2 carrots, chopped

2 celery sticks, chopped

4 garlic cloves, minced

1 onion, chopped

1 teaspoon fresh thyme
leaves

2 tablespoons olive oil

salt and pepper, to taste

FINISHING TOUCHES

150g (5oz) frozen peas

chopped fresh parsley,
to garnish

They say chicken soup is good for the soul as well as the body. It is a go-to dish for anyone feeling under the weather or simply needing a bowl full of comfort and somehow it always does make you feel better! This warming dish is ideally made with fresh, high-quality chicken broth as opposed to stock cubes.

. . . .

1. Add all the main ingredients to a large pot and bring to the boil, before reducing to a medium heat. Cover and cook, stirring often, for 10 minutes.

2. When the chicken is cooked through, remove it and shred with two forks before returning to the pot along with the frozen peas.

3. Simmer for a few more minutes without the lid, to ensure the broth thickens, until the peas have defrosted. Garnish and serve.

Pasta e Fagioli

MAIN INGREDIENTS

750ml (25fl oz) water
  (or use stock and leave
  out the stock cubes)
250g (9oz) ditaloni rigati
  pasta
1½ stock cubes
100g (3½oz) pancetta
  (uncooked)
2 x 400g (14oz) tins pinto or
  borlotti beans, drained
2 x 400g (14oz) tins chopped
  tomatoes
2 carrots, diced
1 onion, chopped
1 red pepper, chopped
2 celery sticks, finely minced
2 tablespoons tomato purée
1 teaspoon dried basil
2 bay leaves
1 teaspoon dried oregano
a few sprigs of fresh thyme
70g (2½oz) Parmesan, grated
salt and pepper, to taste

OPTIONAL GARNISHES

Parmesan cheese, fresh
  thyme, red pepper flakes

This classic Italian dish, which translates simply as 'pasta and beans', originated as a peasant dish due to the cheap ingredients. Today's cooks can still appreciate the frugal nature of the dish, but the real enjoyment will come from the comforting and wholesome flavours. This is the perfect meal for a chilly autumn evening.

. . . .

1. Add all the main ingredients to a large pot and bring to the boil, then reduce to a medium heat and cook, stirring often.

2. Cook until the pasta is al dente and most of the liquid has been absorbed (approximately 15 minutes after boiling). Garnish and serve.

Mac and Cheese ⓥ

MAIN INGREDIENTS

500ml (17fl oz) water
  (or use stock and leave
  out the stock cube)
500ml (17fl oz) whole milk
500g (1lb 2oz) macaroni
1 head of broccoli or
  cauliflower, chopped small
¼ onion, grated
1 stock cube
2 garlic cloves, minced
2 teaspoons Worcestershire
  sauce (use a vegan version
  to make this vegetarian)
1½ teaspoons mustard
  powder
salt and pepper, to taste

FINISHING TOUCHES

180g (6½oz) (or more!)
  Cheddar cheese, grated
50g (2oz) panko-style
  breadcrumbs (optional)

This mac and cheese dish has been the most popular recipe on my blog for quite a few years and is a hit with kids and adults alike. It is shockingly easy to make and yet still somehow better than a traditional recipe. Try this with grated cauliflower for any vegiphobes in your life – they will hardly notice it is there!

. . . .

1. Add all the main ingredients to a large pot and bring to the boil, then reduce to a medium heat and cook, stirring often.

2. Once the pasta is al dente and the liquid mostly absorbed (approximately 15 minutes after boiling), remove from the heat and stir in the cheese.

3. If desired, add more cheese and/or panko-style breadcrumbs to the top of the finished dish, place under a grill and cook until toasty.

Greek Pasta

MAIN INGREDIENTS

500ml (17fl oz) water
  (or use stock and leave
  out the stock cube)
500ml (17fl oz) whole milk
300g (10½oz) rigati pasta
1 stock cube
½ onion, chopped
1 red pepper, chopped
1 green pepper, chopped
1 yellow pepper, chopped
2 garlic cloves, minced
2 tablespoons dried oregano
salt and pepper, to taste

FINISHING TOUCHES

2 large handfuls of spinach,
  chopped
200g (7oz) feta cheese,
  crumbled
kalamata olives, chopped
2 tomatoes, chopped
1 cucumber, chopped
hummus

I came up with this recipe after returning from a trip to Greece when I was looking for a fun, easy way to continue enjoying some of our favourite Grecian flavours. This is particularly delicious when served with a chopped tomato and cucumber salad topped with a spoonful of hummus.

. . . .

1. Add all the main ingredients to a large pot and bring to the boil, then reduce to a medium heat and cook, stirring often.

2. Once the pasta is al dente and the liquid mostly absorbed (approximately 15 minutes after boiling), stir in the spinach, feta and olives (saving a bit of feta to sprinkle on top if desired).

3. Serve with a chopped tomato and cucumber salad topped with hummus.

Pasta Puttanesca

MAIN INGREDIENTS

1 litre (34fl oz) water
   (or use stock and leave
   out the stock cubes)
400g (14oz) spaghetti,
   broken in half
1 aubergine, chopped
200g (7oz) colourful cherry
   tomatoes, halved
2 tablespoons tomato purée
4 garlic cloves, minced
2 teaspoons dried oregano
2 tablespoons olive oil
2 anchovy fillets, minced
1½ stock cubes
50g (2oz) capers
75g (2½oz) pitted
   kalamata olives
salt and pepper, to taste

OPTIONAL GARNISHES

Parmesan cheese, fresh
   parsley, red pepper flakes

This dish may have a very suggestive name in Italian (look it up!) but its pungent, salty flavours make it an absolute classic. Serve with red pepper flakes for an extra kick!

. . . .

1. Add all the main ingredients to a large pot and bring to the boil, then reduce to a medium heat and cook, stirring often.

2. Cook until the pasta is al dente and most of the liquid is absorbed (approximately 15 minutes after boiling). Garnish and serve.

Garlicky Kale and Feta Pasta ⩗

MAIN INGREDIENTS

500ml (17fl oz) water
500ml (17fl oz) whole milk
400g (14oz) fusilli pasta
4 garlic cloves, minced
150g (5oz) kale, chopped
2 tablespoons olive oil
1 teaspoon salt
½ onion, grated
pinch of ground nutmeg
salt and pepper, to taste

FINISHING TOUCHES

juice of ½ lemon
200g (7oz) feta cheese,
    crumbled
50g (2oz) Parmesan cheese,
    finely grated
red pepper flakes, toasted
    pine nuts, lemon wedges,
    to garnish

This recipe is based on my mom's favourite pasta dish, which is bursting with a salty, flavourful Greek cheese called mizithra. While mizithra can be difficult to source, feta makes a delicious alternative! I've paired this dish with garlic and kale to give it a nutritious and flavourful burst.

. . . .

1. Add all the main ingredients to a large pot and bring to the boil, then reduce to a medium heat and cook, stirring often.

2. Once the pasta is al dente and most of the liquid is absorbed (approximately 15 minutes after boiling), stir in the lemon juice, feta and Parmesan. Garnish and serve.

Pasta Primavera

MAIN INGREDIENTS

500ml (17fl oz) water
(or use stock and leave
out the stock cube)
500ml (17fl oz) whole milk
300g (10½oz) linguini,
broken in half
1 stock cube
1 bunch of fresh basil,
chopped
1 onion, chopped
1 bunch of asparagus,
chopped
10 (or so) mushrooms, sliced
4 garlic cloves, minced
2 tablespoons olive oil
squeeze of lemon juice
salt and pepper, to taste

FINISHING TOUCHES

150g (5oz) frozen peas
fried pancetta (which can be
fried first in the same pot
and then removed and set
aside), Parmesan cheese,
to garnish

This is a very versatile recipe perfect for using up any fresh vegetables you have in your fridge. Try using samphire, courgette or sliced Brussels sprouts! Just make sure any dense veg you substitute are grated or cut small to accommodate the cooking time of the pasta.

· ·

1. Add all the main ingredients to a large pot and bring to the boil, then reduce to a medium heat and cook, stirring often.

2. Once the pasta is al dente (approximately 15 minutes after boiling), stir in the frozen peas and cook until all the liquid is absorbed. Garnish and serve.

Baked Gnocchi

MAIN INGREDIENTS

2 x 400g (14oz) tins
  chopped tomatoes

1kg (2lb 4oz) gnocchi

½ onion, grated

3 garlic cloves, minced

2 teaspoons dried oregano

2 teaspoons dried basil

1 teaspoon salt

1 teaspoon sugar

up to ½ tin (200ml/7fl oz)
  water, if needed

salt and pepper, to taste

FINISHING TOUCHES

125g (4oz) fresh mozzarella,
  torn or sliced

Parmesan cheese, to garnish

Baked gnocchi is a fun and delicious dinner, perfect for serving a crowd. This makes a generous portion or provides enough for leftovers the next day. It can also easily be doubled if you have a big enough pot. Try with tortellini for a yummy variation!

1. Add all the main ingredients to a large pot and bring to the boil, then reduce to a low heat. Partially cover with a lid and cook, stirring often.

2. Approximately 15 minutes after boiling, dot the fresh mozzarella over the top. Place under a grill and cook until the cheese is toasty. Garnish and serve.

Antipasto Pasta

MAIN INGREDIENTS

800ml (28fl oz) water
   (or use stock and leave
   out the stock cubes)
400g (14oz) spaghetti,
   broken in half
2 stock cubes
3 garlic cloves, sliced
150g (5oz) marinated
   artichoke hearts,
   roughly chopped
150g (5oz) green and black
   olives, chopped
1 bunch of fresh dill
½ tablespoon dried oregano
1 onion, thinly sliced
400g (14oz) tin chopped
   tomatoes
2 tablespoons olive oil
200g (7oz) cherry tomatoes,
   halved
salt and pepper, to taste

FINISHING TOUCHES

large handful of spinach, chopped
150g (5oz) mini fresh
   mozzarella balls
Parmesan cheese, chopped
   fresh parsley, to garnish

This dish is essentially an antipasto platter in pasta form. What's not to love! Try this with your favourite mix of seasoned olives for an extra-special treat.

· ·

1. Add all the main ingredients to a large pot and bring to the boil, then reduce to a medium heat and cook, stirring often.

2. Cook until the water is mostly absorbed (approximately 15 minutes after boiling), then stir in the spinach and mozzarella balls. Garnish and serve.

Ham and Pea Carbonara

The magic of a carbonara is in the simplicity of the ingredients paired with the creaminess of the egg yolk, yet making this dish can inadvertently leave you with scrambled eggs on pasta … not ideal! I've come up with a foolproof recipe, which is so easy that perhaps you'll forgive the fact that it calls for an extra bowl!

MAIN INGREDIENTS

800ml (28fl oz) water
   (or use stock and leave
   out the stock cubes)
400g (14oz) spaghetti,
   broken in half
2 stock cubes
1 teaspoon salt
250g (9oz) frozen peas
pinch of ground nutmeg
salt and pepper, to taste

FINISHING TOUCHES

1 egg
1 egg yolk
1 large spoonful of crème
   fraîche
90g (3oz) smoked ham batons
   (or chopped ham slices)
75g (2½oz) Parmesan cheese,
   grated
½ teaspoon black pepper
freshly ground black pepper,
   Parmesan cheese,
   to garnish

1. Add all the main ingredients to a large pot and bring to the boil, then reduce to a medium heat and cook, stirring often.

2. Cook until the pasta is al dente but before all the water has been absorbed (about 15 minutes after boiling) as this will give a creamier sauce.

3. Meanwhile, whisk together the egg, egg yolk, crème fraîche, chopped ham and Parmesan with a fork in a small bowl.

4. When the pasta is cooked through, turn off the heat and very quickly stir in the egg/ham mixture until thoroughly incorporated. Garnish and serve.

Creamy Sausage Pasta

MAIN INGREDIENTS

500ml (17fl oz) water
   (or use stock and leave
   out the stock cubes)
500ml (17fl oz) whole milk
400g (14oz) linguine, broken
   in half
2 stock cubes
350g (12oz) sausage meat
   (removed from the casings)
½ onion, chopped
2 garlic cloves, minced
1 red pepper, chopped
salt and pepper, to taste

FINISHING TOUCHES

100g spinach, chopped
1 large spoonful of
   crème fraîche
Parmesan cheese, to garnish

Perfect for a winter's night, it is impossible to have only one bowl of this comforting dish. I like this with a traditional sausage, but it would be delicious with flavoured sausages as well.

. . . .

1. Add all the main ingredients to a large pot and bring to the boil. Reduce to a medium heat and cook, breaking up the sausage and stirring often.

2. Once the pasta is al dente and most of the water is absorbed (approximately 15 minutes after boiling), stir in the spinach and crème fraîche. Garnish and serve.

Chicken Pesto Pasta

MAIN INGREDIENTS

500ml (17fl oz) water
  (or use stock and leave
  out the stock cube)
400ml (14fl oz) whole milk
300g (10½oz) casarecce
  pasta
1 chicken breast
  (approximately 150g/5oz)
1 head of broccoli (just
  the florets), grated
25 cherry tomatoes, halved
1 stock cube
salt and pepper, to taste

FINISHING TOUCHES

3–6 spoonfuls of pesto
Parmesan cheese, fresh basil
  leaves, toasted pine nuts,
  chilli flakes, to garnish

A healthier, heartier version of a traditional 'pasta pesto', this recipe calls for grated broccoli, which blends into the green of the pesto to please even your pickiest eater. Garnish with chilli flakes, toasted pine nuts and freshly grated Parmesan to please grown-ups as well!

· ·

1. Add all the main ingredients to a large pot and bring to the boil, then reduce to a medium heat and cook, stirring often.

2. Once the pasta is al dente and the chicken is cooked through (approximately 15 minutes after boiling), remove and chop the chicken before returning it to the pot.

3. Stir in the pesto and cook until all the liquid is absorbed. Garnish and serve.

Mexican Spaghetti

MAIN INGREDIENTS

800ml (28fl oz) water
(or use stock and leave
out the stock cubes)
300g (10½oz) spaghetti,
broken in half
2 courgettes, chopped
300g (10½oz) chicken breast
400g (14oz) tin black beans,
drained
2 garlic cloves, minced
1 green pepper, chopped
150g (5oz) frozen corn
2 stock cubes
300g (10½oz) jar salsa
1 onion, chopped
2 packages of taco seasoning
salt and pepper, to taste

FINISHING TOUCHES

250g (9oz) Cheddar cheese,
grated
avocado, grated cheese,
spring onions, sliced
black olives, sour cream,
to garnish

I grew up eating as much Mexican food as I did pasta, so combining my two edible passions seemed like an obvious move! This Mexican-inspired dish is a fun and easy way to introduce Mexican flavours to your family.

1. Add all the main ingredients to a large pot and bring to the boil, then reduce to a medium heat and cook, stirring often.

2. Once the pasta is al dente and the chicken is cooked through (approximately 15 minutes after boiling), remove and shred the chicken before returning it to the pot and letting it cook until most of the liquid is absorbed.

3. Sprinkle the finished dish with the cheese and cook under a grill until toasty. Garnish and serve.

Salami Broccoli Pasta

MAIN INGREDIENTS

900ml (30fl oz) water

400g (14oz) farfalle pasta

400g (14oz) tin chopped
  tomatoes

160g (5½oz) sun-dried
  tomato pesto

2 teaspoons salt

2 teaspoons dried basil

2 teaspoons dried oregano

1 head of broccoli,
  chopped small

1 teaspoon salt

FINISHING TOUCHES

100g (3½oz) salami slices,
  chopped

Parmesan cheese, to garnish

The key to this dish is a high-quality salami as that is the ingredient that really makes the entire dish. The result is a bit decadent, but with a good dose of broccoli to make it healthy as well!

. . . .

1. Add all the main ingredients to a large pot and bring to the boil, then reduce to a medium heat and cook, stirring often.

2. Once the pasta is al dente and most of the water is absorbed (approximately 15 minutes after boiling), stir in the salami, garnish with Parmesan and serve.

Sausage and Tomato Pasta

MAIN INGREDIENTS

800ml (28fl oz) water
  (or use stock and leave
  out the stock cubes)
400g (14oz) linguini,
  broken in half
340g (11½oz) sausage
  meat (loose or removed
  from the casings)
400g (14oz) tin chopped
  tomatoes
60g (2oz) sun-dried
  tomatoes in oil, chopped
  (plus 2 tablespoons of
  the oil)
1 onion, chopped
4 garlic cloves,
  very thinly sliced
2 teaspoons dried oregano
2 stock cubes
salt and pepper, to taste

FINISHING TOUCHES

1 bunch of fresh basil,
  chopped
2 handfuls of spinach,
  chopped
Parmesan cheese, fresh basil,
  chilli flakes, to garnish

A rich and delicious take on a traditional meat sauce, this dish is bursting with flavour! The sun-dried tomatoes add depth and interest, while the fresh basil brings a bright freshness to keep the dish from feeling too heavy.

1. Add all the main ingredients to a large pot and bring to the boil. Reduce to a medium heat and cook, breaking up the sausage meat and stirring often.

2. Once the pasta is al dente and most of the water has been absorbed (approximately 15 minutes after boiling), stir in the basil and spinach until wilted. Garnish and serve.

Turkey Tetrazzini

MAIN INGREDIENTS

300ml (10fl oz) water
  (or use stock and leave
  out the stock cubes)
500ml (17fl oz) whole milk
400g (14oz) spaghetti,
  broken in half
300g (10½oz) turkey breast,
  cut into bite-sized pieces
½ onion, grated
2 garlic cloves, minced
100g (3½oz) mushrooms,
  sliced
⅛ teaspoon ground nutmeg
2 stock cubes
salt and pepper, to taste

FINISHING TOUCHES

150g (5oz) frozen peas
80g (3oz) Parmesan, grated,
  plus extra to garnish
150g (5oz) panko-style
  breadcrumbs
Parmesan cheese, fresh
  parsley, sliced black olives,
  to garnish

Turkey tetrazzini is another classic American dish my grandma used to make. Simple and understated, this dish is not dissimilar to an Alfredo, but has slightly more of a bite to it. This recipe is one of my personal favourites. Try serving with a dish of whole black olives, like my grandma always did!

. . . .

1. Add all the main ingredients to a large pot and bring to the boil, then reduce to a medium heat and cook, stirring often.

2. Once the pasta is al dente and most of the liquid is absorbed (approximately 15 minutes after boiling), stir in the frozen peas and parmesan.

3. Add the breadcrumbs to the top of the finished dish and place under a grill until toasty. Garnish and serve.

Creamy Smoked Salmon Pasta

MAIN INGREDIENTS

500ml (17fl oz) whole milk

500ml (17fl oz) water

400g (14oz) tagliatelle

1 leek, cleaned of grit
and chopped

1½ teaspoons salt

salt and pepper, to taste

Not unlike a salmon lox bagel, this dish combines the deliciousness of smoked salmon with a creamy, tangy sauce, making it a classic blend of flavours. Perfect when sprinkled with chopped pistachios!

FINISHING TOUCHES

250g (9oz) trimmed
asparagus, chopped

200g (7oz) smoked salmon,
chopped

120ml (4fl oz) double cream

juice of ¼ lemon

small knob of butter

1 tablespoon chopped
fresh dill

chopped pistachios,
to garnish

1. Add all the main ingredients to a large pot and bring to the boil, then reduce to a medium heat and cook, stirring often.

2. Cook for 5 minutes before adding the asparagus and smoked salmon. Continue cooking over a medium heat until the pasta is cooked through (approximately 15 minutes after boiling), then stir in the cream, lemon juice, butter and dill. Garnish and serve.

Creamy Cajun Prawn Pasta

MAIN INGREDIENTS

500ml (17fl oz) water

500ml (17fl oz) whole milk

400g (14oz) medium shell
   pasta

3 garlic cloves, minced

4 teaspoons Cajun seasoning

1 red pepper, thinly sliced

150g (5oz) cooked smoked
   sausage, sliced

salt and pepper, to taste

FINISHING TOUCHES

300g (10½oz) raw
   king prawns

150g (5oz) spinach, chopped

1 large spoonful of
   crème fraîche

chopped fresh parsley,
   to garnish

This colourful, New Orleans-inspired dish is brimming with flavour. The variety of textures and tastes makes it a fun, unique addition to your weekly meal plan.

1. Add all the main ingredients to a large pot and bring to the boil, then reduce to a medium heat and cook, stirring often.

2. Once the pasta is al dente and most of the water is absorbed (approximately 15 minutes after boiling), add in the prawns, spinach and crème fraîche and stir for 1–2 minutes until the prawns are cooked through. Garnish and serve.

Fish Pie Pasta

MAIN INGREDIENTS

500ml (17fl oz) water
   (or use stock and leave
   out one of the stock cubes)
500ml (17fl oz) whole milk
250g (9oz) garofalo
   cappelletti pasta
200g (7oz) fish pie mix
   (or mix of white fish,
   prawns and smoked fish)
300g (10½oz) potato,
   chopped
1 courgette, chopped
2 carrots, chopped
2 garlic cloves, minced
1 small onion, chopped
2 celery sticks, finely chopped
2 fish stock cubes
3 sprigs of fresh dill
1 bay leaf
salt and pepper, to taste

FINISHING TOUCHES

100g (3½oz) frozen peas
Parmesan cheese or 150g
   (5oz) grated Cheddar
   cheese or 50g (2oz)
   panko-style breadcrumbs
   (optional), to garnish

This is the easiest fish pie you'll ever make! Perfect for a last-minute dinner party or for a bit of comfort food on a quiet night. Either way, this dish is sure to please. Garnish with Parmesan or Cheddar cheese and panko-style breadcrumbs taosted on top!

1. Add all the main ingredients to a large pot and bring to the boil, then reduce to a medium heat and cook, stirring often.

2. Once the pasta is al dente (approximately 15 minutes after boiling), stir in the peas and cook until all the liquid is absorbed.

3. Serve with Parmesan, or the pie would also be great with grated Cheddar or panko-style breadcrumbs on top, toasted under a grill!

Spaghetti and Meatballs

MAIN INGREDIENTS

800ml (28fl oz) water

350g (12oz) fusilli

½ onion, grated

3 garlic cloves, minced

400g (14oz) tin
chopped tomatoes

2 teaspoons dried oregano

2 teaspoons dried basil

1 teaspoon salt

1 teaspoon sugar

2 tablespoons tomato purée

2 tablespoons olive oil

1 package of ready-
made meatballs (about
350g/12oz)

salt and pepper, to taste

OPTIONAL GARNISH

Parmesan cheese

Homemade spaghetti and meatballs is a classic family meal that is easier than ever with my hungerpot method. I've based the sauce on my go-to recipe, which is mild and flavourful. Make this with an extra 50g (2oz) pasta and skip the meatballs for a quick homemade pasta in red sauce!

1. Add all the main ingredients to a large pot and bring to the boil, then reduce to a medium heat and cook, stirring often.

2. Once the pasta is al dente, the meatballs are cooked through and the liquid mostly absorbed (approximately 15 minutes after boiling), remove from the heat, garnish and serve.

Thai Peanut Pasta

MAIN INGREDIENTS

1 litre (34fl oz) water
  (or use stock and leave
  out the stock cubes)
400g (14oz) linguini,
  broken in half
2 stock cubes
1 tablespoon brown sugar
4 garlic cloves, minced
1 tablespoon soy sauce
2 teaspoons fish sauce
1 large carrot, sliced
1 large red pepper, sliced
1 aubergine, chopped
¼ head of broccoli
3 spring onions, thinly sliced
1 large spoonful of
  peanut butter
salt and pepper, to taste

FINISHING TOUCHES

150g (5oz) roasted unsalted
  peanuts
250g (9oz) raw king prawns
fresh coriander, lime wedges,
  chopped peanuts, red
  pepper flakes, sriracha,
  to garnish

Peanut butter may not be a common ingredient in pasta dishes, but it sure makes for a delicious, creamy sauce! I've paired peanut butter with traditional Thai flavours in this recipe for a colourful, veggie-filled dish.

1. Add all the main ingredients to a large pot and bring to the boil, then reduce to a medium heat and cook, stirring often.

2. Once the pasta is al dente and the liquid mostly absorbed (approximately 15 minutes after boiling), add in the peanuts and prawns and stir for 1–2 minutes until the prawns are cooked through. Garnish and serve.

Lasagne Soup

My lasagne soup is a nod to my mom's signature dish: a classic American lasagne. I qualify it as 'American' because my mom makes her lasagne with ricotta cheese instead of a béchamel sauce as it is most commonly made here across the pond. My hungerpot version has all the taste but a fraction of the cheese (the milk base is so creamy it doesn't need it!) and a fraction of the time and effort. I dare you to go back to making a traditional lasagne after trying this one!

MAIN INGREDIENTS

500ml (17fl oz) water
   (or use stock and
   leave out the stock cubes)
500ml (17fl oz) milk
300g (10½oz) mafaldine
   pasta, broken into
   small pieces
100g (3½oz) grated Parmesan
2 chicken stock cubes
1 litre (34fl oz) passata
1 tablespoon olive oil
300g (10½oz) sausage meat
   (removed from casings)
½ onion, chopped
2 garlic cloves, minced
1 tablespoon dried basil
1 tablespoon dried oregano
salt and pepper, to taste

FINISHING TOUCHES

2 handfuls of spinach,
   chopped
1 large spoonful ricotta
   cheese in each bowl
Parmesan cheese, chopped
   parsley, fresh basil,
   to garnish

1. Add all the main ingredients to a large pot and bring to the boil, then reduce to a medium heat and cook, stirring often.

2. Once the pasta is al dente (approximately 15 minutes after boiling), add the chopped spinach and stir until sufficiently wilted. Garnish and serve with a spoonful of ricotta cheese in each individual bowl.

Beef Stroganoff Pasta

MAIN INGREDIENTS

800ml (28fl oz) water
  (or use stock and leave
  out the stock cubes)
400g (14oz) fusilli
230g (8oz) beef (sirloin,
  fillet or rump steak are
  recommended), sliced
  against the grain
2 beef stock cubes
1 onion, chopped
4 garlic cloves, minced
2 tablespoons Worcestershire
  sauce
200g (7oz) mushrooms, sliced
160ml (5½fl oz) dry
  white wine
salt and pepper, to taste

FINISHING TOUCHES

2 large scoops of crème
  fraîche
knob of butter
fresh parsley, black pepper,
  to garnish

I grew up eating my grandma's beef stroganoff and it was always a favourite. Strips of beef and flavourful mushrooms in a rich, creamy sauce … what's not to love! Take a tip from my grandpa and season with lots of black pepper.

1. Add all the main ingredients to a large pot and bring to the boil, then reduce to a medium heat and cook, stirring often.

2. Once the pasta is al dente and the beef is cooked through (approximately 15 minutes after boiling), add the crème fraîche and butter and stir to combine. Garnish and serve.

Lemon Garlic Shrimp and Asparagus Couscous

This light but satisfying dish is ideally served al fresco at the end of a long summer's day. However, given its simplicity and limited ingredients, it is easy enough to throw together any night!

. . . .

MAIN INGREDIENTS

900ml (30fl oz) water

400g (14oz) pearl/Israeli couscous (do not use regular couscous!)

150ml (5fl oz) dry white wine

2 teaspoons salt

4 garlic cloves, minced

juice of ½ lemon

250g (9oz) asparagus, chopped

salt and pepper, to taste

FINISHING TOUCHES

60g (2oz) salted butter

300g (10½oz) raw king prawns

chopped fresh parsley, Parmesan cheese, red pepper flakes, lemon wedges, to garnish

1. Add all the main ingredients to a large pot and bring to the boil, then reduce to a medium heat and cook, stirring often.

2. Once the pasta is al dente and most of the water is absorbed (approximately 15 minutes after boiling), add the butter and prawns and stir until the prawns are cooked through. Garnish and serve.

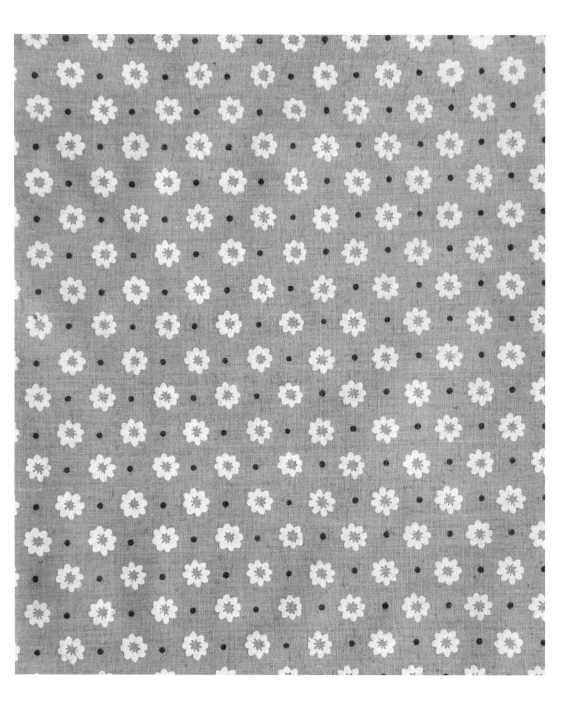

Rice and Noodles

Coconut Lentil Soup

MAIN INGREDIENTS

1 litre (34fl oz) water
  (or use stock and leave
  out the stock cubes)
100g (3½oz) jasmine,
  basmati or long-grain rice
2 stock cubes, crumbled
200g (7oz) split red lentils
400ml (14fl oz) tin
  coconut milk
1 large onion, grated
4 garlic cloves, minced
2 tablespoons grated or
  minced fresh ginger
4 large carrots, chopped
2 teaspoons ground turmeric
½ tablespoon garam masala
½ tablespoon ground cumin
salt and pepper, to taste

OPTIONAL GARNISHES

toasted coconut flakes,
  fresh coriander

This is another hungerpot based on a soup I've been making for years. The result is a warming, creamy bowl of goodness that the whole family will love.

1. Add all the main ingredients to a large pot and bring to the boil over a high heat.

2. Turn down to a medium heat and let simmer until the rice is cooked through and the lentils soft (approximately 15 minutes after boiling). Garnish and serve.

Creamy Chicken Soup with Rice

MAIN INGREDIENTS

1 litre (34fl oz) fresh
   chicken broth or stock
1 litre (34fl oz) whole milk
200g (7oz) jasmine or
   basmati rice
2 chicken breasts, halved
2 carrots, chopped
2 celery sticks, chopped
2 garlic cloves, minced
1 sprig of fresh rosemary
1 small bunch of fresh thyme
salt and pepper, to taste

TO GARNISH

chopped fresh parsley

An absolute classic recipe and still my kids' most requested meal! Search online for the adorable song entitled 'Chicken Soup with Rice' that goes along with the recipe to play while you eat; it makes this lovely dish even more endearing.

1. Add all the main ingredients to a large pot and bring to the boil over a high heat.

2. Turn down to a medium heat and let simmer until the rice is fully cooked (approximately 10–15 minutes after boiling). Remove and shred the chicken before returning it to the pot. Garnish and serve.

Pineapple Cashew Rice

MAIN INGREDIENTS

800ml (28fl oz) water
   (or use stock and leave
   out the stock cubes)
300g (10½oz) jasmine,
   basmati or long-grain rice
260g (9oz) tin pineapple
   chunks, NOT drained
100g (3½oz) raw
   cashew nuts
1½ stock cubes, crumbled
3 tablespoons soy sauce
3 garlic cloves, minced
½ onion, grated
1 carrot, chopped
1 tablespoon honey
1 carrot, chopped
1 green pepper, chopped
salt and pepper, to taste

FINISHING TOUCHES

300g (10½oz) cooked
   frozen prawns
150g (5oz) frozen peas
fresh coriander, sriracha,
   spring onions, to garnish

My favourite Thai restaurant when I lived in Seattle served the most amazing pineapple fried rice, which is the inspiration for this dish. I would order it once a week and swoon over the sweet/salty pairing of the pineapple and soy sauce and the various textures of the veg, prawns and cashews. This is easily vegetarian if you leave out the prawns.

· ·

1. Add all the main ingredients to a large pot and bring to the boil over a high heat.

2. Turn down to the lowest possible heat, cover and cook for 5 minutes before adding the prawns and peas. Let cook for another 5–10 minutes, or until the rice is fully cooked. Garnish and serve.

Tuscan Chicken and Rice

MAIN INGREDIENTS

400ml (14fl oz) water
   (or use stock and leave
   out one of the stock cubes)
400ml (14fl oz) whole milk
200ml (7fl oz) white wine
300g (10½oz) jasmine,
   basmati or long-grain rice
2 chicken breasts, cut
   into bite-sized pieces
1 courgette, sliced
   into thin half-moons
60g (2oz) sun-dried
   tomatoes, chopped (plus
   2 tablespoons of the oil)
1 small onion, grated
2 chicken stock cubes,
   crumbled
2 tablespoons tomato purée
4 garlic cloves, minced
2 sprigs of fresh thyme
1 bunch of fresh basil
salt and pepper, to taste

FINISHING TOUCHES

150g (5oz) baby spinach,
   chopped
Parmesan cheese, fresh basil,
   chilli flakes, to garnish

This dish is best when served on a veranda overlooking the Tuscan countryside … but if that isn't possible, your kitchen table will do – the authentic Tuscan flavours will sweep you away just the same!

1. Add all the main ingredients to a large pot and bring to the boil over a high heat.

2. Turn down to the lowest possible heat, cover and let simmer until the rice is fully cooked (approximately 10–15 minutes after boiling). Stir in the chopped spinach and stir until sufficiently wilted. Garnish and serve.

Spanish Stew

MAIN INGREDIENTS

1 litre (34fl oz) water
   (or use stock and leave
   out the stock cubes)
300g (10½oz) jasmine
   or basmati rice
1 tablespoon olive oil
2 whole chicken breasts
240g (8½oz) chorizo, chopped
1 potato, peeled and diced
2 chicken stock cubes,
   crumbled
½ teaspoon salt
1 tablespoon tomato purée
400g (14oz) tin chickpeas,
   drained
1 tablespoon smoked paprika
pinch of saffron threads
1 onion, grated
4 garlic cloves, minced
1 carrot, chopped
1 red pepper, chopped
salt and pepper, to taste

FINISHING TOUCHES

150g (5oz) frozen peas
fresh parsley, lemon wedges,
   to garnish

Spanish food has always been a favourite of mine and this stew is no exception. The preparation may be as simple as it gets, but the authenticity of the spices and flavours will make this recipe one you will return to again and again. Serve with a hunk of bread for dipping!

1. Add all the main ingredients to a large pot and bring to the boil over a high heat.

2. Turn down to the lowest possible heat, cover and let simmer until the rice is fully cooked (approximately 10–15 minutes after boiling).

3. Remove the chicken and dice before returning to the pot along with the peas. Simmer for a few minutes until the peas have defrosted, then garnish and serve.

Red Beans and Rice

MAIN INGREDIENTS

700ml (24fl oz) water
   (or use stock and leave
   out the stock cubes)
200ml (7fl oz) passata
2 stock cubes, crumbled
300g (10½oz) jasmine,
   basmati or long-grain rice
400g (14oz) tin red kidney
   beans, drained
100g (3½oz) chorizo, diced
1 green pepper chopped
1 onion, minced
2 garlic cloves, minced
1 teaspoon Cajun seasoning
1 bay leaf
salt and pepper, to taste

OPTIONAL GARNISHES

fresh parsley, sliced avocado

Beans and rice are a classic pairing that, when eaten together, make a 'complete protein' (meaning they have the perfect proportions of amino acids for our dietary needs). They also happen to taste great together! This Louisiana-inspired dish is livened up with chorizo to give it an extra burst of flavour.

. . . .

1. Add all the main ingredients to a large pot and bring to the boil over a high heat.

2. Turn down to the lowest possible heat, cover and simmer until the rice is fully cooked (approximately 10–15 minutes after boiling). Garnish and serve.

Caprese Rice

MAIN INGREDIENTS

600ml (20fl oz) water
   (or use stock and leave
   out one of the stock cubes)
500ml (17fl oz) whole milk
300g (10½oz) jasmine
   or basmati rice
2 stock cubes, crumbled
1 tablespoon olive oil
1 small onion, grated
100g (3½oz) Parmesan,
   grated
salt and pepper, to taste

FINISHING TOUCHES

300g (10½oz) cherry
   tomatoes, halved or
   quartered
1 bunch of fresh basil,
   roughly chopped
300g (10½oz) fresh
   mozzarella, cut into
   bite-sized pieces
fresh basil, Parmesan
   cheese, to garnish

A caprese salad (tomato, mozzarella and fresh basil) is an incredibly simple, yet ridiculously tasty combination of flavours. This rice version is lovely and creamy and sure to be a hit with the kids (especially those already fans of a caprese pizza!).

. . . .

1. Add all the main ingredients into a large pot and bring to a boil over a high heat.

2. Turn down to the lowest possible heat, cover and let simmer until the rice is fully cooked (approximately 10–15 minutes after boiling). Stir in the tomatoes, basil and mozzarella. Garnish and serve.

Vegetable Gyoza Rice vg

MAIN INGREDIENTS

900ml (30fl oz) water
   (or use stock and
   leave out the stock cubes)
350g (1oz) jasmine,
   basmati or long-grain rice
1½ stock cubes
5 tablespoons soy sauce
3 garlic cloves, minced
½ onion, grated
1 teaspoon ginger,
   grated or minced
1½ tablespoons honey
1 large carrot, chopped
½ head of broccoli, chopped
salt and pepper, to taste

FINISHING TOUCHES

300g (10½oz) fresh gyoza
Soy sauce, fresh coriander,
   sriracha, spring onions, to
   garnish

I personally find that gyoza are best when steamed, which is how they're cooked in this dish. The dough gets brilliantly chewy and delicious, which I love; steaming gyoza also gets bonus points for being WAY healthier than frying! Throw in some rice and veg and loads of soy sauce and you've got a zinger of a meal.

1. Add all the main ingredients to a large pot and bring to the boil over a high heat.

2. Turn down to the lowest possible heat, cover and cook for 5 minutes before adding the gyoza. Cover and let simmer for another 5–10 minutes, or until the rice is fully cooked and gyoza cooked through. Garnish and serve.

Chicken Katsu Casserole

MAIN INGREDIENTS

800ml (28fl oz) water
   (or use stock and leave
   out the stock cubes)
400ml (14fl oz) tin
   coconut milk
300g (10½oz) jasmine rice
500g (1lb 2oz) chicken thighs
2 stock cubes, crumbled
2 carrots, chopped
1 potato, cubed
3 garlic cloves, minced
1 onion, finely chopped
2 tablespoons soy sauce
3 tablespoons mild
   curry powder
2 teaspoons mirin
2 teaspoons garam masala
salt and pepper, to taste

FINISHING TOUCHES

100g (3½oz) panko-style
   breadcrumbs
fresh coriander, to garnish

Chicken katsu curry is usually served with breaded chicken, but as that isn't possible in a hungerpot, a breadcrumb topping gets the job done instead! As delicious as it is easy, this dish is great for feeding a crowd.

· ·

1. Add all the main ingredients to a large pot and bring to the boil over a high heat.

2. Turn down to the lowest possible heat, cover and simmer until the rice is fully cooked (approximately 10–15 minutes after boiling). Remove and shred the chicken before returning it to the pot.

3. Cover the finished dish with the panko-style breadcrumbs, place under a grill and cook until toasty. Garnish and serve.

Orange Chicken Rice

MAIN INGREDIENTS

750ml (25fl oz) water
  (or use stock and leave
  out the stock cubes)
300ml (10fl oz) orange juice
50ml (2fl oz) light soy sauce
300g (10½oz) jasmine rice
2 chicken stock cubes,
  crumbled
500g (about 6) boneless,
  skinless chicken thighs,
  cut into bite-sized pieces
3 garlic cloves, minced
2 teaspoons grated or
  minced fresh ginger
1 tablespoon sesame oil
2 tablespoons honey
grated zest of 1 orange
salt and pepper, to taste

FINISHING TOUCHES

1 green pepper, chopped
1 red pepper, chopped
1 large handful of green
  beans, chopped in half
toasted sesame seeds, extra
  drizzle of sesame oil, spring
  onions, sriracha, to garnish

A healthier and more delicious take on the classic Chinese dish, this version is boiled instead of fried, making it a fraction of the calories, yet still retaining all the flavour. It also has a generous helping of vegetables, creating a perfect weeknight meal!

. . . .

1. Add all the main ingredients to a large pot and bring to the boil over a high heat.

2. Turn down to the lowest possible heat, stir in the peppers and beans, cover and let simmer until the rice is fully cooked (approximately 10–15 minutes after boiling). Garnish and serve.

Cinnamon Basil Chicken Rice

MAIN INGREDIENTS

500ml (17fl oz) water

300g (10½oz) jasmine, basmati or long-grain rice

1kg (2lb 4oz) chicken drumsticks

2 stock cubes, crumbled

2 tablespoons olive oil

1 onion, chopped

1 tablespoon grated or minced fresh ginger

2 x 400g (14oz) tins chopped tomatoes

3 cinnamon sticks

2 star anise

salt and pepper, to taste

TO GARNISH

chopped fresh basil

This rich, comforting recipe has been a family favourite for years. The cinnamon, basil and ginger make for an absolutely magic combination, which will surely win your hearts as well! This recipe is ideal for feeding a crowd.

· ·

1. Add all the main ingredients to a large pot and bring to the boil over a high heat.

2. Turn down to the lowest possible heat, cover and let simmer until the rice is fully cooked (approximately 10–15 minutes after boiling). Garnish and serve.

Prawn and Broccoli Rice

MAIN INGREDIENTS

600ml (20fl oz) water

500ml (17fl oz) whole milk

300g (10½oz) jasmine,
basmati or long-grain rice

2 stock cubes, crumbled

1 onion, grated

½ tablespoon
smoked paprika

100g (3½oz) Parmesan
cheese, grated

salt and pepper, to taste

FINISHING TOUCHES

1 head of broccoli,
finely chopped

330g (11oz) raw prawns

Parmesan cheese,
fresh basil, to garnish

This recipe is based on a risotto recipe I posted on my blog many years ago. It is a dish we return to over and over again for its simplicity and deliciousness! Made with basmati or jasmine rice instead of arborio, this version is still as creamy but cooks in a fraction of the time!

. . . .

1. Add all the main ingredients to a large pot and bring to the boil over a high heat.

2. Turn down to the lowest possible heat, stir in the broccoli and prawns, cover and simmer until the rice is fully cooked (approximately 10–15 minutes after boiling). Garnish and serve.

Teriyaki Salmon

MAIN INGREDIENTS

900ml (30fl oz) water
  (or use beef stock and
  leave out the stock cubes)
100ml (3½fl oz) soy sauce
100ml (3½fl oz) mirin
300g (10½oz) jasmine,
  basmati or long-grain rice
250g (9oz) skinless salmon
250g (9oz) edamame beans
1½ beef stock cubes,
  crumbled
2 garlic cloves, minced
1 teaspoon grated or minced
  fresh ginger
1 tablespoon honey
salt and pepper, to taste

OPTIONAL GARNISHES

sliced avocado, toasted
  sesame seeds, toasted nori

It is hard not to love a good teriyaki sauce, especially when served with salmon! This simple version is made even more delicious when served with avocado slices on top.

1. Add all the main ingredients to a large pot and bring to the boil over a high heat.

2. Turn down to the lowest possible heat, cover and let simmer until the rice is fully cooked (approximately 10–15 minutes after boiling). Garnish and serve.

Orange Basil Cod and Rice

MAIN INGREDIENTS

700ml (24fl oz) water
  (or use stock and leave
  out the stock cubes)
120ml (4fl oz) white wine
300g (10½oz) jasmine or
  basmati rice
1½ chicken, fish or veg stock
  cubes, crumbled
1 garlic clove, minced
zest and juice of 1 orange
  (about 120ml/4fl oz juice)
1 tablespoon olive oil
200g (7oz) spinach, chopped
1 bunch of fresh basil,
  chopped
250g (9oz) cod fillet
salt and pepper, to taste

OPTIONAL GARNISHES

lemon wedges, chopped fresh
  basil, drizzle of olive oil

A bright, fun dish for a summer evening, the pairing of citrus and white fish is a classic combo. Serve with a nice glass of chilled white wine.

. . . .

1. Add all the main ingredients to a large pot and bring to the boil over a high heat.

2. Turn down to the lowest possible heat, cover and let simmer until the rice is fully cooked (approximately 10–15 minutes after boiling). Garnish and serve.

Mujaddara 🌱

MAIN INGREDIENTS

1 litre (34fl oz) water
   (or use stock and leave
   out the stock cubes)
200g (7oz) brown lentils
200g (7oz) basmati rice
2 stock cubes, crumbled
2 garlic cloves, minced
1 onion, finely chopped
½ teaspoon ground cinnamon
½ teaspoon ground cumin
salt and pepper, to taste

FINISHING TOUCHES

60ml (2fl oz) tahini
juice of ½ lemon
dried onions, sliced tomatoes
   and cucumbers, chopped
   fresh parsley, drizzle of olive
   oil, to garnish

This popular Middle Eastern dish was first recorded in a cookbook in 1226! Sometimes made with beef, this vegetarian version is an easy, flavourful dish for any night of the week.

. . . .

1. Add all the main ingredients to a large pot and bring to the boil over a high heat.

2. Turn down to the lowest possible heat, cover and let simmer until the rice and lentils are fully cooked (approximately 15 minutes after boiling).

3. Meanwhile, mix the tahini with the lemon juice and a big pinch of salt in a small bowl to make the tahini sauce.

4. Serve the mujaddara drizzled with the tahini sauce and plenty of garnishes!

Garlic Mushroom Rice ⓥ

MAIN INGREDIENTS

500ml (17fl oz) water
  (or use stock and leave
  out one of the stock cubes)
400ml (13fl oz) whole milk
200ml (7fl oz) white wine
300g (10½oz) jasmine
  or basmati rice
1½ stock cubes, crumbled
250g (9oz) mushrooms, sliced
10g (½oz) dried
  wild mushrooms
1 small onion, grated
4 garlic cloves, minced
2 sprigs of fresh thyme
100g (3½oz) Parmesan,
  grated
salt and pepper, to taste

FINISHING TOUCHES

300g (10½oz) trimmed
  asparagus, chopped
Parmesan cheese, to garnish

The mild flavours of this dish really allow the mushrooms and asparagus both to shine. This is best made during asparagus season, when you can buy it locally grown!

· ·

1. Add all the main ingredients to a large pot and bring to the boil over a high heat.

2. Turn down to the lowest possible heat, cover and let simmer for 7 minutes. Stir in the asparagus, then cover again and continue cooking until the rice is cooked through (about 3–8 more minutes). Garnish and serve.

Lamb Biryani

MAIN INGREDIENTS

700ml (24fl oz) water

300g (10½oz) basmati rice

300g (10½oz) diced leg
  of lamb

2 stock cubes, crumbled

½ tin (200g/7oz) chopped
  tomatoes

2 tablespoons tomato purée

2 tablespoons olive oil

1 teaspoon grated or
  minced fresh ginger

1 onion, grated

3 garlic cloves, minced

1 teaspoon garam masala

1 teaspoon ground turmeric

¼ teaspoon fennel seeds

½ star anise

1 cinnamon stick

salt and pepper, to taste

FINISHING TOUCHES

2 handfuls of spinach,
  chopped

mango chutney, natural
  yoghurt, chopped fresh
  coriander, to garnish

We rarely had lamb when I was a kid because my mom claimed it stunk up the entire house. So as a result, my lamb-loving dad made it whenever she was out of town! Ha! That being said, this lamb biryani would please even my mother as the fragrant aroma as it cooks is divine. Serve with mango chutney and some naan bread for an impressive-looking dinner party meal.

. . . .

1. Add all the main ingredients to a large pot and bring to the boil over a high heat.

2. Turn down to the lowest possible heat, cover and let simmer until the rice is fully cooked (approximately 10–15 minutes after boiling). Stir in the spinach until wilted, then garnish and serve.

Mongolian Beef Rice

MAIN INGREDIENTS

900ml (30fl oz) water
(or use beef stock and
leave out the stock cubes)
500g (1lb 2oz) beef (sirloin,
fillet or rump steak are
recommended), sliced
against the grain
100ml (3½fl oz)
light soy sauce
300g (10½oz) jasmine rice
2 beef stock cubes, crumbled
50g (2oz) soft light brown
sugar
3 garlic cloves, minced
2 teaspoons grated or minced
fresh ginger
2 teaspoons sesame oil
1 head of broccoli, chopped
into small pieces
1 carrot, chopped
salt and pepper, to taste

OPTIONAL GARNISHES

sesame seeds, chopped
spring onions

Mongolian beef has long been a favourite dish of mine. The sweet, yet super-savoury sauce will hook you on the first bite! The beef cooks up nicely using this method, but the best part for me is always the broccoli because it picks up so much of the delicious sauce!

1. Add all the main ingredients to a large pot and bring to the boil over a high heat.

2. Turn down to the lowest possible heat, cover and simmer until the rice is fully cooked (approximately 10–15 minutes after boiling). Garnish and serve.

Turkey Broccoli Rice Casserole

MAIN INGREDIENTS

500ml (17fl oz) water
  (or use stock and leave
  out one of the stock cubes)
550ml (18fl oz) whole milk
300g (10½oz) jasmine,
  basmati or long-grain rice
1 head of broccoli, chopped
300g (10½oz) turkey breast,
  cut into bite-sized pieces
2 garlic cloves, minced
2 stock cubes, crumbled
1 teaspoon chicken seasoning
salt and pepper, to taste

FINISHING TOUCHES

200g (7oz) Cheddar or
  Gruyère cheese, grated
  (more if you're a
  cheese person!)
1 packet of seasoned
  breadcrumbs
cranberry sauce, to serve

Based on my favourite casserole, which my mom makes, this dish is an American classic. Though the original recipe calls for cream of chicken soup, this version successfully relies on the creaminess of the rice and a bit of milk instead, making it still delicious, but much healthier! Serve with cranberry sauce on the side for some sweet/salty magic.

. . . .

1. Add all the main ingredients to a large pot and bring to the boil over a high heat.

2. Turn down to the lowest possible heat, cover and let simmer until the rice is fully cooked (approximately 10–15 minutes after boiling).

3. Stir in the cheese, then cover the finished dish with breadcrumbs, place under a grill and cook until toasty. Serve with cranberry sauce.

Kung Pao Noodles

MAIN INGREDIENTS

450ml (16fl oz) water
(or use stock and leave
out the stock cube)
1 stock cube, crumbled
500g (1lb 2oz) chicken breast,
cut into bite-sized pieces
75ml (3fl oz) soy sauce
5 garlic cloves, sliced
150ml (5fl oz) white wine
3 spoonfuls of chilli paste
small knob of fresh ginger,
minced
½ red pepper, sliced
200g (7oz) green beans
1 tablespoon toasted
sesame oil
1 teaspoon white sugar
salt and pepper, to taste

FINISHING TOUCHES

300g (10½oz) dried
Chinese egg noodles
sesame seeds, sriracha,
chopped peanuts, spring
onions, to garnish

This spicy dish can be made in less time than it would take for you to order a takeaway! And because the version is simmered instead of stir-fried, it makes for a much healthier option as well.

. . . .

1. Add all the main ingredients to a large pot and bring to the boil, before reducing to a medium heat and leaving to simmer for 10 minutes for the flavours to blend together.

2. Add the egg noodles amd simmer for a futher 4–5 minutes until cooked through. Garnish and serve.

Miso Noodle Soup

MAIN INGREDIENTS

2 litres (70fl oz) cold water

200g (7oz) dried Chinese
  egg noodles

3 tablespoons red or white
  (milder) miso paste

1 stock cube, crumbled

2 eggs (raw and whole
  in the shell)

100g (3½oz) mushrooms,
  sliced

200g (7oz) edamame beans

150g (5oz) smoked tofu,
  chopped

salt and pepper, to taste

FINISHING TOUCHES

80g (3oz) mangetout

spring onions, sesame seeds,
  sriracha, sliced onion,
  toasted nori, to garnish

It is hard not to love the mild, salty flavour of miso soup. I've beefed this version up with noodles, lots of veg, smoked tofu and even some hard-boiled eggs, which cook at the same time as everything else!

1. Add all the main ingredients to a large pot and bring to the boil, before reducing to a medium heat and cooking, stirring often (carefully so as not to break the eggs).

2. Simmer for 15 minutes, or until the noodles are al dente. Once the noodles are cooked, add the mangetout and simmer for 1 minute.

3. Remove, peel and halve the eggs and then add back to the pot. Garnish and serve.

Pho

MAIN INGREDIENTS

2 litres (70fl oz) water
 (or use stock and leave
 out the stock cubes)
3 beef stock cubes, crumbled
1 tablespoon fish sauce
2 garlic cloves, minced
1 small onion, chopped
1 teaspoon grated or
 minced fresh ginger
1 star anise
pinch of ground cinnamon
1 tablespoon olive oil
salt and pepper, to taste

FINISHING TOUCHES

200g (7oz) thin rice noodles
1 bunch of pak choi, chopped
juice of 1 lime
100g (3½oz) roast
 beef slices
beansprouts, fresh basil, fresh
 coriander, fresh mint, sliced
 fresh chilli, sriracha, lime
 wedges, to garnish

Pho is a traditional Vietnamese soup best known for its incredibly flavourful broth and bright garnishes (so don't scrimp on your selection). A favourite for kids and grown-ups alike, this dish is as colourful as it is delicious!

. . . .

1. Add all the main ingredients to a large pot and bring to the boil. Simmer for 10 minutes to allow the flavours to blend together.

2. Add the noodles and pak choi and simmer for a few minutes, then stir in the lime juice. Add the slices of beef to each bowl, garnish generously and serve.

Plants and Beans

Corn Chowder

MAIN INGREDIENTS

300ml (10½fl oz) water

300ml (10½fl oz) whole milk

400g (14oz) frozen sweetcorn

1 small onion, grated

1 celery stick, chopped

1 carrot, chopped

1 potato, cubed

100g (3½oz) pancetta, diced

1 stock cube

salt and pepper, to taste

FINISHING TOUCHES

100g (3½oz) Cheddar cheese,
    grated

fresh chives, fried pancetta
    (which can be fried first
    in the same pot and then
    removed and set aside),
    to garnish

This sweet and creamy chowder is sure to delight kids and grown-ups alike. Serve topped with crumbled streaky bacon for a decadent treat!

· ·

1. Add all the main ingredients to a large pot and bring to the boil, then reduce to a medium heat and cook, stirring often.

2. Simmer until the veg is cooked through (approximately 15 minutes after boiling). Use a hand blender to blend to the desired consistency, then mix in the grated cheese or sprinkle on each bowl individually. Garnish and serve.

Brown Lentil Soup vg

MAIN INGREDIENTS

1.5 litres (52fl oz) water
   (or use stock and leave
   out the stock cubes)
400g (14oz) brown lentils
3 stock cubes
4 garlic cloves, minced
1 large onion, chopped
4 carrots, cut into small pieces
4 celery sticks, finely chopped
1 tablespoon olive oil
1 tablespoon ground cumin
1 small bunch of fresh thyme
1 bay leaf
salt and pepper, to taste

FINISHING TOUCHES

large handful of
   spinach leaves
fresh parsley, to garnish

This lentil soup may not look like much, but the flavours come together so beautifully that it is always a hit with kids and adults alike. I serve this with a rolled tortilla or parathas on the side. Make this with a vegetable broth for a wonderfully hearty vegan meal.

. . . .

1. Add all the main ingredients to a large pot and bring to the boil, then reduce to a medium heat and cook, stirring often.

2. Simmer until the lentils are soft (approximately 40 minutes after boiling). Stir in the spinach until wilted. Remove from the heat and use a hand blender to purée the soup, adding more water if needed. Garnish and serve.

Potato Leek Soup

MAIN INGREDIENTS

1 litre (34fl oz) water
(or use stock and leave
out the stock cubes)

2 stock cubes

2 tablespoons butter

2 tablespoons olive oil

4 large leeks, cleaned of grit
and diced (just the white
and light green parts)

4 large potatoes, peeled and
chopped

salt and pepper, to taste

OPTIONAL GARNISHES

chopped spring onions,
chopped fresh herbs

Unlike traditional potato leek soup recipes, which call for cream, this recipe relies on the creaminess of the potato to get the job done, and it sure does. This is a perfect soup for freezing and pulling out midweek!

· ·

1. Add all the main ingredients to a large pot and bring to the boil, then reduce to a medium heat and cook, stirring often.

2. Simmer until the veg is cooked through (approximately 15 minutes after boiling). Use a hand blender to blend to the desired consistency. Garnish and serve with crusty bread.

Sweet Potato Chilli v

MAIN INGREDIENTS

500ml (17fl oz) water

1 large sweet potato, peeled and cubed

1 onion, chopped

1 green pepper, chopped

4 garlic cloves, minced

2 teaspoons chilli powder

1 tablespoon ground cumin

1½ tablespoons unsweetened cocoa powder

2 teaspoons Worcestershire sauce (use vegan version to make this vegetarian)

1 teaspoon ground cinnamon

2 x 400g (14oz) tins chopped tomatoes

400g (14oz) tin black beans, drained

400g (14oz) tin kidney beans, drained

1 teaspoon salt

salt and pepper, to taste

OPTIONAL GARNISHES

sour cream or Greek yoghurt, spring onions, sliced radishes, tortilla chips

This dish is one that is definitely more fun with a variety of garnishes (radishes, tortilla chips, Greek yoghurt …) but the depth of flavours the cinnamon and cocoa powder add make it delicious on its own as well. If feeding this to kids, start with just half a teaspoon of chilli powder and add more to the adult portions later. Smoked paprika can also be used instead if need be. Serve this with my cornbread recipe opposite.

· ·

1. Add all the main ingredients to a large pot and bring to the boil, then reduce to a medium heat and cook, stirring often.

2. Simmer until the veg is cooked through (approximately 15 minutes after boiling). Garnish and serve.

Cornbread

50g (2oz) salted butter

100g (3½oz) sugar

150g (5oz) polenta

1 teaspoon baking powder

2 eggs

125ml (4fl oz) crème fraîche

250ml (8½fl oz) whole milk

150g (5oz) plain flour, sifted

Cornbread is not a staple in the UK as it is in the US (especially in the South), but I intend to single-handedly change that with this recipe. Commonly served alongside a bowl of chilli (or at the top or bottom of a bowl of chilli), it is also incredible on its own with a pad of butter and/or honey.

1. Preheat the oven to 200°C (400°F).

2. On the hob, melt the butter in an ovenproof pan, then remove from the heat before mixing in the ingredients in order.

3. Bake for 20 minutes, or until a knife inserted in the centre comes out clean.

Peanut Butter Lentils vg

MAIN INGREDIENTS

200g (7oz) split red lentils

200g (7oz) jasmine, basmati or long-grain rice

2 spoonfuls of peanut butter (around 80g)

1 tablespoon grated or minced fresh ginger

3 garlic cloves, minced

2 tablespoons soy sauce

juice of ½ small lime

4 stalks of fresh coriander, chopped

400ml (14fl oz) tin coconut milk

½ teaspoon salt

1 tablespoon sugar

1 tablespoon sesame oil

1 small onion, sliced

1 red pepper, sliced

1 large carrot, chopped into half moons

1 courgette, chopped into half-moons

salt and pepper, to taste

OPTIONAL GARNISHES

fresh basil, sriracha

Peanut butter lentils have been a favourite in our house for years. Not only is this dish filled with loads of veg, it is also completely vegan, getting its creaminess from the peanut butter and coconut milk. This is delicious topped with sriracha!

1. Add all the main ingredients to a large pot and bring to the boil, then reduce to a medium heat and cook, stirring often.

2. Simmer until the veg is cooked through and the lentils soft (approximately 15 minutes after boiling). Garnish and serve.

Moroccan Stew

MAIN INGREDIENTS

600ml (20fl oz) water

400g (14oz) tin chickpeas,
    drained

1 onion, chopped

400g (14oz) tin
    chopped tomatoes

2 garlic cloves, minced

1 yellow or red pepper,
    chopped

4 carrots, diced

180g (6½oz) quinoa, rinsed

50g (2oz) raisins

2 tablespoons honey

4 sprigs of thyme

2 teaspoons ground turmeric

1 teaspoon ground cinnamon

2 teaspoons ground coriander

2 tablespoons ground cumin

1–2 teaspoons paprika

salt and pepper, to taste

OPTIONAL GARNISHES

fresh coriander, plain
    yoghurt, toasted almonds,
    pistachios, harissa,
    red pepper flakes

I have long been a fan of the flavours and textures of Moroccan food. The use of fruit and fresh herbs, the fluffiness of a perfectly cooked couscous and the deliciousness of a slow-cooked tagine are all hard to beat. While not technically a tagine (which is named after the clay pot used for cooking), my version incorporates the traditional flavours and textures of a traditional tagine. Be sure to add in some garnishes (the toasted almonds are my favourite!) for extra texture and flavour!

1. Add all the main ingredients to a large pot and bring to the boil, then reduce to a medium heat and cook, stirring often.

2. Simmer until the vegetables are soft (approximately 25 minutes after boiling), remove from the heat, garnish and serve.

Cuban Picadillo

MAIN INGREDIENTS

600ml (20fl oz) water
  (or use stock and leave
  out one of the stock cubes)
300g (10½oz) brown lentils
100g (3½oz) jasmine, basmati
  or long-grain rice
2 stock cubes
3 garlic cloves, minced
1 onion, chopped
1 red pepper, chopped
1 potato, peeled and cubed
400g (14oz) tin chopped
  tomatoes
2 tablespoons tomato purée
50g (2oz) green olives, sliced
½ teaspoon ground cinnamon
2 teaspoons ground cumin
pinch of ground nutmeg
1 bay leaf
50g raisins
salt and pepper, to taste

TO GARNISH

fresh coriander

The pairing of olives and raisins may seem unexpected, but alongside the other flavours it just works! Best enjoyed with a large Cuban cigar on the side (just kidding).

. . . .

1. Add all the main ingredients to a large pot and bring to the boil, then reduce to a medium heat and cook, stirring often.

2. Simmer until the lentils are soft (approximately 40 minutes after boiling). Garnish and serve.

Smoked Paprika Lentil Soup ⚥

MAIN INGREDIENTS

1.5 litres (52fl oz) water
(or use stock and leave
out the stock cubes)

250g (9oz) split red lentils

50g (2oz) bulgur wheat

3 stock cubes

1 tablespoon olive oil

1 large onion, finely chopped

2 sprigs of fresh thyme

3 garlic cloves, minced

1 tablespoon tomato purée

1½ teaspoons sweet
smoked paprika

salt and pepper, to taste

FINISHING TOUCHES

150g (5oz) spinach leaves,
chopped

Greek yoghurt, to garnish

This recipe has been a staple in our family for many years and is a go-to meal when we've otherwise run out of groceries! I've simplified the original (pulled from a newspaper!) but maintained the basic idea, which really lets the onion and smoked paprika shine.

1. Add all the main ingredients to a large pot and bring to the boil, then reduce to a medium heat and cook, stirring often.

2. Simmer until the lentils are soft (approximately 15 minutes after boiling) and stir in the spinach. Garnish and serve.

Cannellini Bean and Ham Soup

MAIN INGREDIENTS

800ml (28fl oz) water
  (or use stock and leave
  out the stock cubes)
2 x 400g (14oz) tins
  cannellini beans, drained
1½ stock cubes
2 garlic cloves, minced
2 carrots, chopped
1 celery stick, chopped
1 large onion, chopped
150g (5oz) smoked gammon,
  diced
salt and pepper, to taste

FINISHING TOUCHES

1 spoonful of butter
fresh thyme, fresh parsley,
  to garnish

'Pork and beans' (called 'frank and beans' when made with hot dogs!) is a classic dish from America's South. Also try this with black-eyed beans for a delicious, though less creamy-tasting, option.

1. Add all the main ingredients to a large pot and bring to the boil, then reduce to a medium heat and cook, stirring often.

2. Simmer until the veg is cooked through (approximately 10–15 minutes after boiling). Remove from the heat and stir in the butter. Garnish and serve.

Gigantes Plaki

MAIN INGREDIENTS

2 x 400g (14oz) tins butter
   beans, drained

2 x 400g (14oz) tins cannellini
   beans, drained

1 tablespoon tomato purée

1 stock cube

3 garlic cloves, minced

2 carrots, chopped

1 celery stalk, minced

1 onion, chopped

1 tablespoon olive oil

1 teaspoon brown sugar

1 teaspoon dried oregano

2 teaspoons dried dill

1 bay leaf

½ teaspoon ground cinnamon

salt and pepper, to taste

OPTIONAL GARNISHES

fresh parsley, drizzle of olive
   oil, chilli flakes

Made mostly of items you can find in your cupboard, this fragrant and spice-filled dish is a Greek classic. It is particularly lovely with a piece of crusty bread and an extra drizzle of olive oil at the end. And not only is this dish gluten free, but when made with vegetable broth, it is also vegan!

. . . .

1. Add all the main ingredients to a large pot and bring to the boil, then reduce to a medium heat and cook, stirring often.

2. Simmer until the veg is cooked through (approximately 15 minutes after boiling). Garnish and serve.

Chicken Pot Pie

MAIN INGREDIENTS

680ml (23fl oz) water

120ml (4fl oz) white wine

600g (1lb 5oz) whole chicken
breasts

2 carrots, diced

2 celery sticks, diced

2 garlic cloves, minced

1 onion, grated

6 sprigs of fresh thyme

salt and pepper, to taste

FINISHING TOUCHES

60g (2oz) room-temperature
unsalted butter

60g (2oz) plain flour

150g (5oz) frozen peas

100ml (3½fl oz) double cream

ready-rolled shortcrust pastry
dough

1 egg, beaten, for brushing
the pastry

Chicken pot pies were a favourite meal of mine as a kid. Between the sauce and the pastry, I hardly even noticed how many vegetables I was consuming! Kids love helping with this version using cookie cutters for the dough.

. . . .

1. Preheat the oven to 200°C (400°F).
2. Add all the main ingredients to a large pot and bring to the boil, then reduce to a medium heat and cook, stirring often.
3. Simmer until the chicken and vegetables are cooked through. Meanwhile, mash together the butter and flour to a paste and set aside.
4. Remove the chicken and dice or shred, according to your preference, then return to the pot along with the frozen peas and butter-flour mixture.
5. Simmer over a medium heat, stirring constantly, for about 2 minutes until the sauce is thickened. Stir in the cream and season to taste with freshly ground black pepper.
6. Unroll the pastry and cut out into shapes. Brush each piece with beaten egg. The pastry can then be placed directly over the pie mixture (leaving some gaps so steam can escape) or cooked on a separate baking sheet and placed on each serving individually. Bake for 20–25 minutes until the pastry is golden brown all over.

Feta and White Bean Shakshuka ⓥ

MAIN INGREDIENTS

2 x 400g (14oz) tins white
beans, drained

2 stock cubes

4 garlic cloves, minced

1 large onion, chopped

2 x 400g (14oz) tins chopped
tomatoes

50g (2oz) kale, chopped

1 teaspoon smoked paprika

1 teaspoon ground cumin

1 teaspoon dried oregano

1 tablespoon olive oil

salt and pepper, to taste

FINISHING TOUCHES

4–8 eggs (depending on
the diameter of your pot)

crumbled feta cheese,
chopped fresh coriander,
red pepper flakes,
to garnish

This dish is as beautiful as it is delicious.
Serve with crusty bread and cheese for a quick
and easy dinner party meal!

. . . .

1. Add all the main ingredients to a large
   pot and bring to the boil, then reduce to
   a medium heat and cook, stirring often.

2. Simmer until the veg is tender (approximately
   15 minutes after boiling). Remove from the
   heat and use the back of a spoon to create
   wells in the mixture to crack eggs into.

3. Add the eggs, place under a grill and cook
   until the eggs reach their desired doneness.
   Garnish and serve.

Beef Stew

MAIN INGREDIENTS

750ml (25fl oz) water
250ml (8½fl oz) red wine
700g (1lb 9oz) casserole beef
2 beef stock cubes
8 sprigs of fresh thyme
1 onion, grated
2 garlic cloves, minced
3 carrots, chopped
2 celery sticks, chopped
500g (1lb 2oz) small potatoes,
    halved or quartered
    (depending on size)
1 teaspoon Worcestershire
    sauce
2 tablespoons tomato purée

FINISHING TOUCHES

30g (1oz) room-temperature
    butter
30g (1oz) plain flour
salt and pepper, to taste
fresh parsley, to garnish

A winter staple, this traditional beef stew is great for making ahead and freezing. It is a perfect way to warm up at the end of a chilly day!

. . . .

1. Add all the main ingredients to a large pot and bring to the boil, then reduce to a medium heat and cook, stirring often.

2. You can eat this the moment the vegetables are cooked through, or you can let it continue to simmer over a low heat for several hours, until the beef is very tender.

3. When you're ready to serve, mash the butter and flour together into a paste and stir into the simmering stew. It should thicken within a couple of minutes. Season to taste with salt and pepper. Garnish and serve.

Plants and Beans

Sweet Potato Stout Stew vg

MAIN INGREDIENTS

600ml (20fl oz) water
(or use stock and leave
out one of the stock cubes)
500ml (17fl oz) Irish stout beer
2 stock cubes
4 sweet potatoes, peeled
and cubed
1 onion, diced
3 garlic cloves, minced
2 carrots, chopped
1 parsnip, chopped
250g (9oz) cabbage,
cut into thin strips
2 sprigs of fresh thyme
1 dried bay leaf
1 teaspoon fennel seeds
salt and pepper, to taste

TO GARNISH

fresh parsley

This dish is a bit of an enigma, but don't worry, it is a delicious enigma! I've taken a traditional Irish stout stew, removed the beef, swapped around some ingredients and voilà: we're left with a flavourful stew full of veg and beer. What's not to love?

1. Add all the main ingredients to a large pot and bring to the boil, then reduce to a medium heat and cook, stirring often.

2. Simmer until the veg is cooked through. Garnish and serve.

Aubergine and Cannellini Caponata ⱱ

MAIN INGREDIENTS

500ml (17fl oz) water

2 x 400g (14oz) tins
cannellini beans, drained

1 x 400g (14oz) tin chopped
tomatoes

1 large aubergine, chopped

1 red pepper, chopped

1 sprig of fresh oregano

1 onion, chopped

2 tablespoons capers

60g (2oz) pitted green olives,
chopped

1 teaspoon red wine vinegar

2 garlic cloves, minced

2 tablespoons tomato purée

2 tablespoons olive oil

2 teaspoons salt

salt and pepper, to taste

OPTIONAL GARNISHES

chopped fresh parsley,
grated Parmesan cheese,
crumbled feta cheese

This caponata is a delicious and healthy stew, perfect for an autumn evening. Mix up this Italian dish by serving it with hummus!

· ·

1. Add all the main ingredients to a large pot and bring to the boil, then reduce to a medium heat and cook, stirring often.

2. Simmer until the veg is cooked through (approximately 15 minutes after boiling). Garnish and serve.

Mushroom Bourguignon ⓥ

MAIN INGREDIENTS

500ml (17fl oz) water
250ml (8½fl oz) red wine
2 mushroom or veg stock cubes
750g (1lb 10oz) various fresh
    mushrooms, washed and
    chopped (I recommend
    250g/9oz portobello,
    250g/9oz shiitake and
    250g/9oz chestnut
    mushrooms)
2 large carrots, chopped
3 garlic cloves, minced
1 onion, grated
6 sprigs of fresh thyme
1 bay leaf
2 tablespoons tomato purée

FINISHING TOUCHES

30g (1oz) room-temperature
    unsalted butter
30g (1oz) plain flour
salt and pepper, to taste
chopped fresh parsley,
    to garnish

Fill your umami quota with this hearty stew! Serve over mashed potatoes, a baked potato or on its own with a hunk of bread.

1. Add all the main ingredients to a large pot and bring to the boil, then reduce to a medium heat and cook, stirring often.

2. Simmer until the veg is cooked through (approximately 15 minutes after boiling).

3. Meanwhile, mash the butter and flour together into a paste.

4. Once the veg is cooked, stir the butter-flour paste into the stew and simmer for about 1 minute until thickened. Season to taste with salt and pepper. Garnish and serve.

Hungerpuds

Apple Cobbler ♥

MAIN INGREDIENTS

75g (2½oz) salted butter

3 tablespoons white sugar

2 tablespoons plain flour

½ tablespoon ground
cinnamon

pinch of ground nutmeg

½ teaspoon vanilla extract

75g (2½oz) oats

50g (2oz) brown sugar

FINISHING TOUCHES

5 apples, cored and sliced

Both nutritious and delicious, this apple cobbler is as easy as it gets. Leave the peel on the apple for extra fibre! Serve with vanilla ice cream or custard.

· ·

1. Preheat the oven to 200°C (400°F).

2. Melt the butter in a large ovenproof cast-iron pan before adding the rest of the main ingredients. Stir until well mixed, then gently fold in the apples.

3. Bake for approximately 10 minutes, or until the apples are softened and the top is toasty.

Skillet Brownies

125g (4oz) unsalted butter

100g (3½oz) dark chocolate, finely chopped

200g (7oz) white sugar

¼ teaspoon salt

1 teaspoon vanilla extract

2 eggs

85g (3oz) plain flour

100g (3½oz) milk chocolate chips (or other small milk chocolate pieces)

Once you try these brownies, you will never go back to a box mix! It took me countless variations to get this recipe to the fudgey side of delicious, but I promise you this will make the easiest and most deliciously gooey batch of brownies ever! Serve with vanilla ice cream.

1. Preheat the oven to 180°C (350°F).
2. Melt the butter in an ovenproof cast-iron frying pan on the stove. Add the chocolate and stir to melt. Remove from the heat once the butter and chocolate are melted. Using a rubber spatula, stir in the sugar, salt and vanilla and mix well. (If not using cast-iron, it is best to then pour the mixture into a buttered pan).
3. Whisk the eggs on their own (easiest with a fork) before stirring into the mixture. Sift in the flour and mix well before gently stirring in the chocolate chips (allowing some to remain unmelted). Use the spatula to scrape the sides of the pan clean.
4. Cook for 30–40 minutes, or until a knife comes out mostly clean. These are meant to still be fairly gooey in the middle, so the knife won't be completely clean!
5. Let rest for 5–10 minutes before eating, ideally with a big scoop of vanilla ice cream on the side!

Coconut Chai Rice Pudding ⱽ

MAIN INGREDIENTS

1 litre (34fl oz) whole milk

200g (7oz) jasmine, basmati or long-grain rice (pudding rice is possible, but takes longer)

1 teaspoon ground cinnamon (or 1 cinnamon stick)

¼ tsp salt

115g (4oz) white sugar

2 teaspoons vanilla extract

30g (1oz) butter

5g (¼oz) piece of peeled fresh ginger, left whole

1 star anise

⅛ teaspoon ground nutmeg

⅛ teaspoon ground cloves

pinch of black pepper

30g (1oz) raw coconut flakes

OPTIONAL GARNISHES

ground cinnamon, toasted coconut flakes

A fun and flavourful take on the original, this rice pudding makes for a delicious weeknight treat.

· ·

1. Add all the main ingredients to a pot and cook together, over a medium heat, stirring often, until the rice is cooked. Long-grain rice should take around 15 minutes and pudding rice around 45 minutes. If using pudding rice, use half the amount of ginger as it releases more flavour as it cooks.

2. Remove the ginger, then garnish and serve.

# Fried Bananas ⱽ

MAIN INGREDIENTS

60g (2oz) unsalted butter

130g (4½oz) soft dark
   brown sugar

1 teaspoon vanilla extract

2 teaspoons almond extract

½ teaspoon ground cinnamon

50g (2oz) chopped walnuts

FINISHING TOUCHES

3 ripe bananas, each cut
   in half, then sliced in
   half lengthways

juice of ¼ lemon

A traditional Bananas Foster calls for setting rum on fire in your saucepan … this much simpler (and safer!) version forgoes the alcohol and fire, but is just as delicious! Perfect topped with a scoop of vanilla ice cream.

1. Melt the butter over a medium heat before mixing in all the other main ingredients.

2. Once mixed, gently fold in the banana, making sure it is well coated, and let cook for 3–5 minutes.

3. Squeeze in the lemon juice and gently mix. Serve with vanilla ice cream.

Blueberry Bread Pudding ♥

MAIN INGREDIENTS

45g (1½oz) salted butter
1 tablespoon vanilla extract
300g (10½oz) golden syrup
500ml (17fl oz) whole milk
6 eggs

FINISHING TOUCHES

¾ crusty loaf (about 600g/1lb
    5oz), cut into 2.5cm (1 inch)
    cubes
400g (14oz) fresh or
    frozen blueberries
maple syrup or custard
    and icing sugar, to garnish

Made with fresh or frozen blueberries, this dish serves up a huge hit of antioxidants. Great as a pudding or a special breakfast treat (you can make it the night before and store in the fridge).

. . . .

1. Preheat the oven to 200°C (400°F).

2. On the hob, melt the butter in an ovenproof pan. Remove from the heat before whisking in the main ingredients in order.

3. Gently fold in the bread, making sure it is fully soaked through before folding in the blueberries. You can prep up to this point ahead of time and let it sit for up to 10 hours in the fridge like this.

4. Bake for 25–30 minutes, or until cooked through and toasty on top. Garnish and serve.

Crazy Cakes vg

Kids will love helping you make these bizarre cakes, which are egg and dairy free but made with vinegar! Crazy cake (also called 'depression cake') originated in the 1930s out of necessity, but continues to be well loved due to its super-simple, yet absolutely delicious recipe. I'm including the traditional chocolate recipe as well.

. . . .

Pineapple Crazy Cake

275g (10oz) plain flour

200g (7oz) white sugar

1 teaspoon bicarbonate of soda

½ teaspoon salt

1 teaspoon white distilled vinegar

2 teaspoons vanilla extract

5 tablespoons vegetable oil

250ml (8½fl oz) juice from the tin of pineapples, topped up with water

1 tin pineapple rings (save the juice!)

3 tablespoons maple syrup

1. Preheat the oven to 180°C (350°F).
2. Combine all the dry ingredients in an ovenproof pan.
3. Using your knuckle, make three wells in the mixture. Add the vinegar in one well, the vanilla in another well and the vegetable oil in the third well.
4. Pour the juice/water mixture over the top of all the ingredients and mix well (I find this works best with a fork when done in the pan).
5. Arrange the pineapples on the top before drizzling the cake with maple syrup (being sure to cover the pineapple). Bake for 30–35 minutes, covering halfway through with foil if needed.

Chocolate Crazy Cake

275g (10oz) plain flour

30g (1oz) unsweetened cocoa
   powder

200g (7oz) white sugar

1 teaspoon bicarbonate of
   soda

½ teaspoon salt

1 teaspoon white distilled
   vinegar

1 teaspoon vanilla extract

5 tablespoons vegetable oil

250ml (8½fl oz) water

1. Preheat the oven to 180°C (350°F).

2. Combine all the dry ingredients in an
   ovenproof pan.

3. Using your knuckle, make three wells in the
   mixture. Add the vinegar in one well, the
   vanilla in another well and the vegetable oil in
   the third well.

4. Pour the water over the top of all the
   ingredients and mix well (I find this works best
   with a fork when done in the pan).

5. Bake for 30–35 minutes.

Peach Crazy Cake

275g (10oz) plain flour
200g (7oz) white sugar
1 teaspoon bicarbonate
   of soda
1 teaspoon ground cinnamon
½ teaspoon salt
1 teaspoon white distilled
   vinegar
2 teaspoons vanilla extract
5 tablespoons vegetable oil
250ml (8½fl oz) juice from
   the tin of peaches,
   topped up with water
1 tin peach slices
3 tablespoons maple syrup

1. Preheat the oven to 180°C (350°F).

2. Combine all the dry ingredients in an ovenproof pan.

3. Using your knuckle, make three wells in the mixture. Add the vinegar in one well, the vanilla in another well and the vegetable oil in the third well.

4. Pour the juice/water mixture over the top of all the ingredients and mix well (I find this works best with a fork when done in the pan).

5. Add the peach slices before drizzling the cake with maple syrup (being sure to cover the peaches). Bake for 30–35 minutes, covering halfway through with foil if needed.

Notes

Notes

Notes

Notes

© James Eppy

About the Author

About the Author

Hi! I'm Bethie (short for Elizabeth). I am an American and British mother of two who loves singing, travelling, crafting and cooking. I was born and raised in a small farming town north of Seattle in Washington State and spent eight years in Washington, D.C. before arriving in London (with a newborn baby) in 2011. Nine years and another baby later, I am now a single/co-parenting mum living in South East London.

Having degrees in both music and social work, I never imagined I would end up making my career in food; though looking back, it seems to have been an obvious choice all along. My parents still talk about how much I enjoyed food as a baby and anyone who has eaten with me as an adult also knows how much I love food (as does anyone nearby, ha!) because I can't stay quiet about it. I will 'mmmm' and 'oh my goodness' until my fellow diners tell me to tone it down. (Yes, I'm one of those people!)

I have also been a professional singer for the last twenty years. I specialise in Renaissance and Early Baroque music but sing everything from chant to jazz to indie pop. You can find my album *Love and Lust* on iTunes by searching 'Elizabeth Hungerford'.

I would love for you to join me on Instagram where you can find me at @hungermama. I share everything from recipes to interior decorating inspiration and daily share my 'three good things' as a reminder that we can always find joy if we're looking for it. Please also check out my podcast 'Friends with Recipes', where I go into people's homes and get them to cook their favourite recipe for me. (I also dig through their cupboards and refrigerators, so it's a lot of fun!)

Thank you all for joining me on my culinary journey! I am genuinely thrilled to have each of you along for the ride.

Index

Page references in *italics* indicate images.

A note on the props

We were thrilled to have so many gorgeous vintage pots and props to work with on this shoot. To make things even more special, many of the items included in the book were borrowed from my own home, such as the vintage cookbook on page 9 that was given to me by my mom when I was 18. Other special items include my grandparents' salt and pepper shakers, which they always kept on their dining table, a painted rooster, cookie cutters, tea towels, table cloths, skillets and basically anything else fun and charming I could find from my personal collection. Additionally, my friend Charlotte Bland, who photographed the book, provided some special items from her own home, such as her grandma's table cloth. These special personal touches make the book feel even more unique and charming to me – and I hope they will for you as well!

Acknowledgements

To my children, Charlotte Loveday and Peter Thomas Hungerford, for being constant sources of love and inspiration.

To my parents, Karen and Greg Peterka, for their devotion and love.

To my siblings Brian Peterka and Annie Boucher and families.

To Jason Hungerford for his encouragement and support.

To Barb Abbott, who sparked my love for cooking.

To Tina Hawes for the joy and creativity she so freely shared.

To Ross Mathews for his encouragement, support and being an unending source of joy.

To Molly Fitterer and Kate Davies for their unconditional love and friendship.

To Christine Buras who helped me test many a recipe.

To my lovely neighbours (Celia, et al), who tested so many dishes for me.

To Sarah Archard for her guidance and friendship.

To Nina Weinreich for being an absolute rock in my life.

To Julia Knott for her love and support.

To Po Chen for his friendship.

To Susie Kavinski and Jessica Irish for their friendship.

To Father David Brant for his friendship and support.

To Katie Abbott for her love and support.

To the Dawson family
for all of the love.

To Katharine Richardson
for being my advocate.

To Lydia Good for believing in me.

To Tas Braithwaite for her
love and support.

To Melissa Hemsley for her support.

To Charlotte Bland for her
friendship and kindness.

To Pippa Leon for her
prowess in the kitchen.

To Emily Quinton for her loveliness,
kindness and support.

To all of my podcast guests
for their time and talent.

To 'The Nice Girl's Club' for their
friendship and encouragement.

To Kari Cartwright for her
friendship and light.

To Hannah Mallatratt
for her support.

To Peter Thomas Reynolds for
being an absolute darling.

To my sixth grade teacher Mrs
Scott, who made me promise
when I was 12 that I would
dedicate my first book to her.
I hope this is good enough!

I would like to give an especially
big thank you to all of my
incredibly supportive and all-
around wonderful followers on
social media. I would not have had
the opportunity to write this book
if it weren't for you all. Thank you
from the bottom of my heart.